Zak and Lex Get Cod

By Carmel Reilly

Zak and Lex get in a van.

The van zips to the dam.

Cod is in the dam.

Cod is yum!

cod

Zak gets a rod
and a big net.

Lex has a box.

box

net

rod

The sun is up,
so Zak pops on a hat.

hat

Lex gets the rod.

Lex looks for cod.

Lex tugs on the rod.

But it is **not** a cod.

Lex can see a tin can!

tin can

CHECKING FOR MEANING

1. Where did Zak and Lex go in the van? *(Literal)*

2. What type of fish is in the dam? *(Literal)*

3. Why did Lex think he had caught a cod? *(Inferential)*

EXTENDING VOCABULARY

zips	Explain that *zips* can have two different meanings. Ask students to use the words in a sentence to show their different meanings. Which one is used in the text?
box	What is a *box*? What is another word that has the same meaning? If you take away the *b*, which other letter can go at the start to make a new word?
can	What are two different meanings of the word *can* in the sentence: *Lex can see a tin can!*? Explain that the first one means Lex is able to see, and the second is a container made from tin.

MOVING BEYOND THE TEXT

1. Have you ever been fishing? Did you catch any fish?

2. What do you need to catch a fish? What is used to make the fish come up to the hook?

3. What do you think Lex had in his fishing box?

4. What are the names of some different fish?

SPEED SOUNDS

Xx	Yy	Zz		
Kk	Ll	Vv	Qq	Ww
Dd	Jj	Oo	Gg	Uu

Cc	Bb	Rr	Ee	Ff	Hh	Nn
Mm	Ss	Aa	Pp	Ii	Tt	

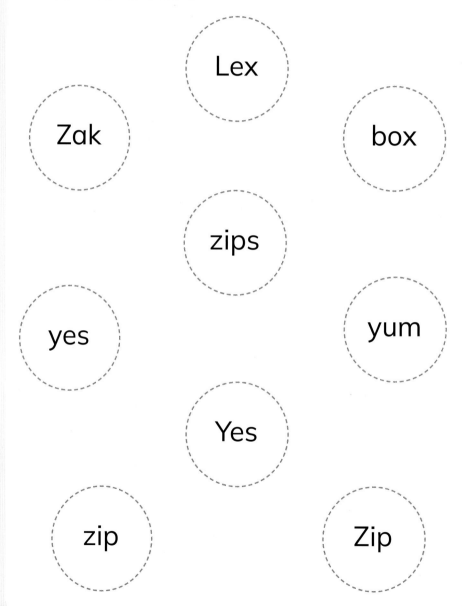

Lex

Zak

box

zips

yes

yum

Yes

zip

Zip